The Novello Book of Carols

The Novello
Book of Carols

compiled and edited by
William Llewellyn

NOVELLO PUBLISHING LIMITED
8/9 Frith Street, London W1V 5TZ

to my family
and in our affectionate remembrance of
Warren Green

A M D G

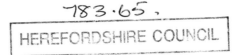
Part One Cat. No. 05 0046 ISBN 0 85360 125 9

Part Two Cat. No. 05 0047 ISBN 0 85360 126 7

Complete Cat. No. 05 0048 ISBN 0 85360 127 5

Cover illustration *I Re Magi* (S. Apollinare Nuovo, Ravenna)
© Scala/Firenze Reproduced by permission

Cover design by Malcolm Harvey Young FSIAD, MSTD

Contents

Introduction

When I was invited to produce suggestions for a comprehensive new Christmas carol collection, I was delighted to be able to draw on over 35 years' experience of organizing and directing Carol Concerts and Services. Having had to produce many arrangements of my own to suit many varied choral and instrumental demands – both amateur and professional – my initial file of ideas grew rapidly and this Novello Book of 90 Carols is the result.

16 carols and a further 39 arrangements are published here for the first time.

Carols from France, Holland, Germany, Italy, Czechoslovakia, and Canada, are included, and the three carols from Spain I obtained from Snr Enrique Ribo following a concert tour to Barcelona with the Linden Singers. Three of my own arrangements were written in Italy, and a visit to Ravenna inspired the idea for the cover illustration.

69 carols are suitable for unaccompanied singing; the Index shows this. Further, it is often useful to have readily available alternative settings – in mood, style, length, or scoring – of the same words, and 14 of these are included. The provision of Performing Notes is indicated by *PN* at the head of the music where applicable.

The book runs mainly in alphabetical order under first lines of English text, but we have made a few changes to try to keep repeated sections on facing pages and to avoid awkward turns forward or back.

Orchestral parts and full scores for 24 of the carols are obtainable on hire; details of the orchestrations, and much other useful information, will be found in the comprehensive Index at the end.

This Novello Book of Carols (NBC) is also the parent book for The Novello Junior Book of Carols (NJBC) which contains 21 pieces from it. The arrangements, all compatible with NBC, have Chime Bars, School Percussion, two Melody Parts (each in C & B flat), Guitar chords, Bass Line, and simplified Piano. They make possible joint Concerts and Services with Schools and Adult Choirs; the full orchestral scores include all the school parts.

I am most grateful to all musical contributors: to James Woodhouse, Headmaster of Lancing College, for his skill in finding words which create so successfully atmosphere, sound, and meaning: to my colleague, Robin Totton, for his help with the Catalan texts: and especially to Robin Langley, Publisher to Novello & Company, for his acute perception and for his untiring interest and industry; without him, and Leslie Ellis with the expert team of technical staff, this book would never have come into being.

Charterhouse, 1986   *William Llewellyn*

Performing Notes

The carols are listed alphabetically under first lines

NO. PAGE

1 1 ⎫
2 2 ⎬ *A babe is born.* Each version lilts gently, with a considerable dynamic range overall, and some freedom in the unison refrains. With four voices only, omit Alto 1 and Bass 1 in the last few bars of each version.

4 6 *A little child there is yborn.* This should be taken at a steady pace so that all the quavers can be articulated – they should be crisp and detached, not smooth. It will go very well at ♩.= 92, but could be sung faster, up to ♩.= 104.

6 14 *Ancient prophets first foretold him.* This is undoubtedly a March, and the men should sound like a brass band; a good 'm' at the end of each 'Fum' will help to make the effect. The upper voices are also part of the marching procession – perhaps as children running and dancing round the band as it marches through the streets.

5 9 *As I walked down the road.* The humming accompaniment moves serenely throughout the opening. The word 'Star' (bar 26) can form a real climax, and can be matched in exhilaration by the word 'shining'.

10 22 *As Joseph was a-walking.* Serene and dignified. Verses 2 and 4 may have different soloists. The 'Mm' may have half-closed lips if this suits the acoustics.

7 16 *Away in a manger.* Even-sounding throughout, with no *crescendi* or *rallentandi* to disturb the gentle flow, and with no hint of pauses between verses. In contrast to this, the final humming surges and grows, before receding to the very soft finish.

8 18 *Blessed be he that cometh.* The 'Ah' at the beginning of each section starts confidently and then 'makes room' for the hints of plainsong which it supports. The rhythmic pulse of the Refrain makes a good contrast.

75 229 *Born in the night.* The words tell you precisely the expression needed. The layout here is explained under carol 74, p.viii, 'The First Nowell'. 'Born in the night' also sounds well between verses of 'Hark! the herald angels sing' – use two verses of 'Born in the night' each time; either transpose the carol down (to F), or up (to A flat).

9 20 *Christmas is coming.* This can have real outdoor carol style. Walford Davies once explained that in bars 5 and 6 ('hat____') the old man is poking his hat at the passers-by. There is a chance of a spectacular *crescendo* at the end of bar 13. The traditional tune at the end will take a rustic, almost clumsy, treatment with the quavers heavier than usual. And the final unison E flat can really ring.

14 30 *De Virgin Mary had a baby boy.* Plenty of West Indian swing, and a sense of good humour can emerge. 'Duh', not 'Dee'. The dynamic contrasts should be large.

13 29 *Ding-dong, ding.* There is an alternative 'Rondo Route' through this carol and it balances well. Sing straight through the whole page with only the first set of words; straight through again, but with the second set of words; finish with the opening line. The words ''tis no fable' sound well sung very softly, as a one-bar aside.

15 34 *Ding dong! merrily on high (i).* To avoid the usual trap of 'Hosanna-rin excelsis' I asked the choir to add a rest, and the 5/4 time seemed to follow naturally.

17 37 *Donkey plod and Mary ride.* This is adapted from Eric Thiman's unison song, 'The Path to the Moon'. The carol-like quality of the tune made me look for suitable words; these by Timothy Dudley-Smith might easily have been written specially for this tune.

19 44 *Dormi Jesu. (ii).* Very calm and serene, with a feeling of a tune in each of the three parts: the cadences all have major triads and there is an opportunity for beautiful, glowing chords.

22 50 *God rest you merry, gentlemen.* This should be full of *bonhomie* and energy. The last few bars should be taken by storm.

20 46 *Hark, the herald angels sing.* Mendelssohn's 'Festgesang' (scored for male chorus and brass, and originally having no connection with Christmas) supplies the opening fanfare. The barring is his also.

21 49 *Hodie, hodie Christus natus est.* This can make an excellent start for a Carol Service or Concert. There are two possible endings to suit the keys of the carol or hymn following.

23 57 *How soft, upon the ev'ning air.* Many pieces of music have one bar or one section which suggests the speed appropriate for the whole. Here it is the bar of 'See how he sleeps'; this has a hint of both repose and movement. If this bar is at the right speed for the acoustic of the place in which you are singing, the whole will sound good.

24 60 *Hushaby low.* The chorus should be very restrained throughout, and particularly when accompanying the soprano at the beginning. Here the solo voice should be thrown into relief as though the Madonna were illuminated by a single candle in a darkened room.

25 63 *Hush you, my baby.* At bar 69 the plural word SOLOISTS asks for a soprano voice and a man's voice together. You could use more than one of each voice, but each octave should be there. It would be possible to sing the whole carol to the music of verse 2.

26 66 *I'm a-ridin' to Bethlehem.* The trotting horse ('Troc-a-tron') approaches, goes past, and away, all in a few seconds. The hard 'c' clicks in each bar, the quaver (-a-) has its own energy and the 'n' of 'tron' must be heard clearly. Though the tune comes from Czechoslovakia, you may like to try a touch of mid-Western accent. At the end of the piece no hint of slowing, but simply sounding further away until out of earshot. Your own tempo will depend on the two words 'trot quickly' and how well they sound in your acoustic.

29 76 *In the bleak mid-winter (i).* This may be sung very thoughtfully: in verse 3 (. . .'thronged the air'), the heavenly celebrations should be very loud; the singers then sing very softly without any break so that the next words 'but only his mother' are 'discovered' as the loud phrase dies away.

30 80 *In the bleak mid-winter (ii).* Verse 3 can be very effective with solo soprano accompanied by humming choir. The parts for strings and wind can be used as interludes between the sung verses.

28a 72 ⎰
28b 74 ⎱ *In this most joyful night.* This arrangement of a most evocative tune is never loud – the intensity of the notes is carried up to the ends of phrases more than in our own English tradition; this brings out the elusive quality of the song.

31 81 *In thy mother's arms.* I found this lullaby in Rome and have used it frequently. The soloist sings gently above the rocking accompaniment. A little extra weight in the last bar (C flat) for the choir will help the finish, but the general mood never changes.

33 86 *I saw three ships (ii).* When John Wilson asked me to make an arrangement of this I asked, 'Which of the two well-known tunes shall I use?' His answer was 'Both!' It is quite easy to run the two different tunes at your own chosen speeds; the last few bars should be quite fast and almost 'thrown away', with the speed maintained to the final bar.

34 89 *I sing of a maiden.* Serene, using the simple resonances of the chords. With four voices only, omit Bass 1 in bars 10 and 10a.

35 90 *Jerusalem rejos for joy.* There is a great deal of atmosphere here with majesty and mystery combined, and possibilities of rich texture and colouring. 'Ch' is pronounced as in Scottish 'loch'; 'Jerusalem' and 'josit' each have a hard 'j'.

38 99 *Joy to the world (ii).* There is so much of Handel's character in this strong tune that it seemed natural to clothe the three verses with Handelian accompaniments and interludes. There are some easily-recognisable quotations in the added parts.

39 104 *King Jesus hath a garden.* Always gentle and soothing; the hints of flutes and other instruments are obvious but always miniature. This garden is sunny and contains a great variety of colour.

43 116 *Lully, lulla (ii).* In this arrangement the refrain comes only at the beginning and at the end. As well as the 3/4 time there are sections which should be sung as if they are in 3/2 and 6/8. The 6/8 in particular should be strongly rhythmical.

45   120   *Mary's Child, so new and fair.* The contraltos rock the cradle all the time. There is an echo, shown by the figures I and II, implicit in the tune (and in James Woodhouse's words). You may obtain this echo effect by distance or you may create it from within the choir. There is a real climax, but the piece is always intimate, starting almost imperceptibly and fading away to nothing at the end.

44a   118 }
44b   119 } *Mary, Mother of God's dear child.* Very busy and energetic. The accents on 'Oh' in contralto, tenor, and bass can be featured. Verse 3 can be extremely quiet, with a real contrast when the *ff* final verse comes. In Spain they sing the last few bars so loudly and triumphantly that you forget your fears about waking the baby.

50   140   *Nowell, Nowell, Who is there?* Plenty of accent and robust quavers all through both the refrains and the tune sections; the final 'Nowell' should be flung out as a challenge.

53   156   *Now is Christemas ycome.* Sing buoyantly with much rhythmic verve. The repeated chords (as in bar 7) should be very full, but also clear and precise. The quavers after the ties (e.g. 'fere' in bar 10) have no length, and so the final consonant comes on the beat.

55   164   *O come, all ye faithful.* If you do not wish to sing verse 6 ('born this happy morning') you can use the setting of it for any other verse (though you will probably wish to make it your final one).

57   170   *O magnum misterium.* Each 'choir' can be replaced by an organ or by an accompanying group. Parts are available on hire for brass instruments. The characteristic richness of the writing will still be heard. The triple-time 'Alleluia' should sound very lively and buoyant.

59   184   *Once in royal David's city.* The traditional treatment of the opening verse as a solo may, of course, be adopted. For unaccompanied use, the words of verse 6 may be sung to the A.H. Mann setting on the opposite page.

60   186   *O my dear heart (ii).* A third verse, hummed *pp*, helps to carry the carol's special serenity.

63   196   *Past three o'clock (ii).* This may be performed in two different ways: you may sing the whole piece, or simply bars 32-120. This arrangement is a reminder that these are the London Waits, with the watchman calling the time as the clock chimes − no-one heeds him; and the next section is slow, with distant carol singers approaching. At bar 32 the singers have arrived; keep this part bright and lively, bringing out each carol tune as it comes. In the 'Good King Wenceslas' section, one (at most two) baritones sing bass. Their voices should be heard only as a means of deepening and thickening the tenor-bass sound. An off-stage horn where marked (a hint of 'Die Meistersinger'?) can be effective. The horn player plays from the vocal score at concert pitch.

The dynamic range of a real bell is huge − a loud clang, dying away very rapidly, turning slowly into a humming sound which slowly dies away. A hard 'D' on the 'Don' will help; and you may get different bell timbres by inviting various 'bell-singers' to use a different vowel sound (French 'Din' is an example'). The final bell-sound goes on for a long time and you can let it fade into the surrounding resonance.

65   204   *Rejoice lordings.* This should be sung with a great deal of word-energy, and in a very direct manner from beginning to end. The last bars give no hint that you are ending and should take the listener by surprise.

66   209   *See him born.* Think of a Gavotte, with firm accents on the first of the bar, and the piece will dance. Sing 'le diveen-enfant'. The humming should be nasal, buzzing, to imitate the sound and drone of pipes or French hurdy-gurdy.

67   212 }
68   213 } *See, to us a child is born.* The antiphon effect can be obtained by using two groups, one singing the words in roman type, the other those in italics.

71   220   *Sweet was the song the Virgin sang.* Each of the three 'La-lu-la' sections is more expansive than the one before; the time-signatures indicate this.

72   223   *The angel Gabriel.* This arrangement dances just a little. It may be sung unaccompanied by ignoring the interludes and lengthening the last chord in verses 1-3.

74   228   *The first Nowell.* The descants are optional and can be used in any verse. The second descant (verse 4 onwards), with its cross-rhythm, is the more energetic in style.

To make a real finish to a Carol Service it is always possible to 'sandwich' one carol inside another. 'Born in the night' sung during 'The First Nowell' is a good example and it is printed here so that you may sing either carol separately, or follow the order of the printed pages. The opening of the unaccompanied verses must be carefully rehearsed.

If a congregation is to join in singing the special setting of the last verse, a congregational rehearsal will obviously be desirable.

76   234   *The holly and the ivy.* The solo voice may be a treble or a tenor, each singing in alternate verses. The organ may play with the choir, but it must play its own part in bars 12-15. A second group of singers, or congregation, may sing the tune of the refrain.

78   238   *There is no rose of such virtue.* There are opportunities here for matching the parts when singing together or in canon, with a beautiful and serene ending.

84   256   *Tyrle, tyrlow.* These words are pronounced as if made up of three syllables and split to sound 'ty-re-leh, ty-re-low'. The musical rhythm throughout must be

Ty-re-le,   ty-re-low

86   264   *Villagers all, this frosty tide.* This is the Carol of the Field-Mice, and a reading from Kenneth Grahame's 'The Wind in the Willows' makes a good introduction.

83   253   *What shall we give?* The speed should be set so that the semi-quavers receive considerable weight and become almost heavy. This is not a rocking carol. In the last verse the unusual long-held F sharp should be insistent until finally it becomes part of the last chord; the voices singing 'non' should do so emphatically and with intensity.

88   270   *Worship the Christ-child.* The three choirs may be three quartets and the canon will sound well if the groups are spaced apart. The organisation is very simple; each choir enters as soon as the previous one reaches the asterisk. Thus each choir sings through each verse once (the same music three times) and then adds the short Coda (here called 'Verse 4'). Performed in this way, Choir 1 begins alone for the first bar-and-a-half and Choir 3 finds itself singing the Coda alone at the finish. There is an obvious climax in the middle.

1. A BABE IS BORN (i)

Words traditional
English 15th century

ROBIN WELLS

1. A babe is born all of a may,* To bring sal-va-tion un-to us. To him we sing both night and day: Ve-ni cre-a-tor Spi-ri-tus.

2. At Beth-le-hem, that bless-ed place, The child of bliss now born he was; And him to serve God give us grace, O lux be-a-ta Tri-ni-tas.

3. There came three kings out of the East, To wor-ship the King that is so free, With gold and myrrh and frank-in-cense, A so-lis or-tus car-di-ne.

4. The shep-herds heard an an-gel's cry, A mer-ry song that night sung he. 'O why are ye so sore a-ghast?' Jam or-tus so-lis car-di-ne.

5. The an-gels came down with one cry, A fair song that night sung they, To join in wor-ship of that child: Glo-ri-a ti-bi Do-mi-ne.

after last verse pp Glo - ri-a ti-bi, Do - mi - ne.

Mm, mm.

* maid

for Farnham and Bourne Choral Society

2. A BABE IS BORN (ii)

Words traditional
English 15th century

ROBIN WELLS

1. *p* A babe is born all of a may,* To bring sal-
3. *mp* There came three kings out of the East, To wor-ship the

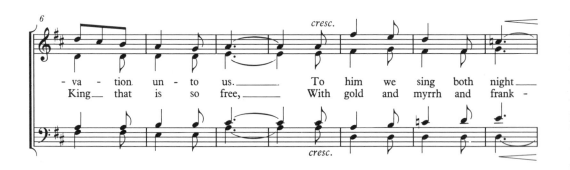

- va-tion un-to us. To him we sing both night
King that is so free, With gold and myrrh and frank -

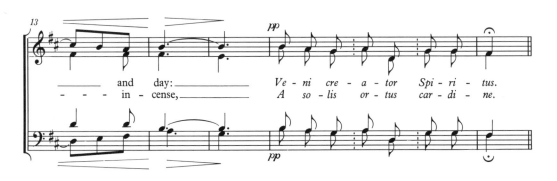

and day: Ve - ni cre - a - tor Spi - ri - tus.
- - in - cense, A so - lis or - tus car - di - ne.

2. *mp* At Beth - le - hem, that bless - ed place, The child of bliss now
4. *mf* The shep - herds heard an an - gel's cry, A mer - ry song that

* maid

© Copyright 1986 Novello & Company Limited

3. ADAM LAY YBOUNDEN

Words anon. 15th century

BORIS ORD

Allegretto ♩=108

SOPRANO ALTO

1. A - dam lay y - bound - en, Bound - en in a bond;

TENOR BASS

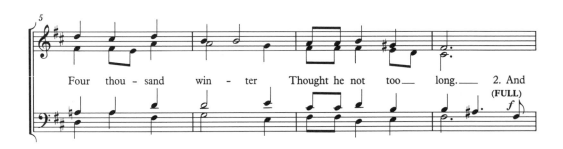

Four thou - sand win - ter Thought he not too— long.— 2. And

(FULL)

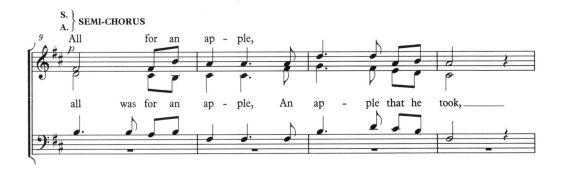

S. A. } SEMI-CHORUS

All for an ap - ple,

all was for an ap - ple, An ap - ple that he took,—

As clerk - es find - en Writ - ten in their book.

B. SEMI-CHORUS

* must

4. SUSANNI

A little child there is yborn

Words anon. 15th century

RONALD CORP

Words collated by Percy Dearmer (1867–1936); from the *Oxford Book of Carols* by permission of Oxford University Press

5. THE LITTLE ROAD TO BETHLEHEM

As I walked down the road

Words by
MARGARET ROSE

MICHAEL HEAD

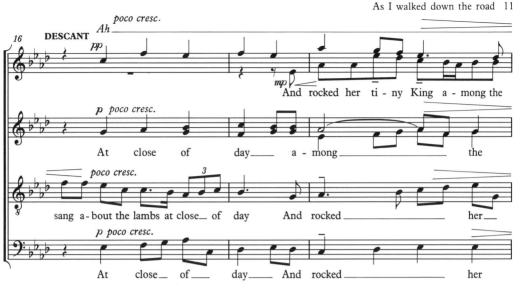

6. FUM, FUM, FUM

Ancient prophets first foretold him

Words anon.

Traditional Spanish carol
arranged by WILLIAM LLEWELLYN

7. AWAY IN A MANGER

Words anon.

Tune by W. J. KIRKPATRICK
arranged by WILLIAM LLEWELLYN

8. DAWN CAROL

Blessed be he that cometh

Gradual and Alleluia in the second
Mass of Christmas, The Mass of Dawn

MALCOLM WILLIAMSON

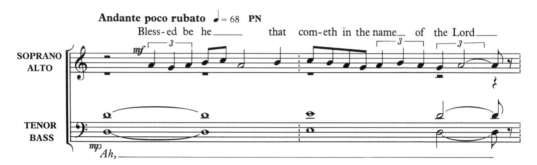

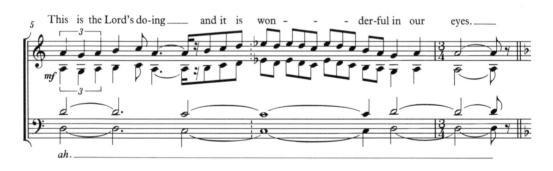

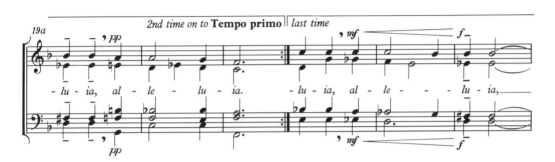

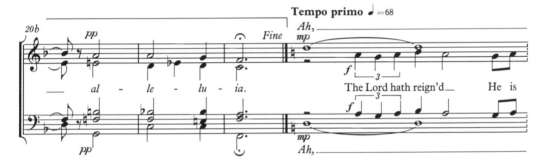

9. CHRISTMAS IS COMING

Words traditional

WALFORD DAVIES
using traditional melody
for final stanza

10. AS JOSEPH WAS A-WALKING

Words traditional

Traditional tune from Rimbault:
Old English Carols (1865)
arranged by ROBIN WELLS

for Cecily Smithwick and the East Coker W.I.

11. THE OXEN

Words by
THOMAS HARDY

Christmas Eve

BENJAMIN BRITTEN

12. A SOMERSET CAROL

Come all you worthy people here

Words traditional
(slightly adapted)

English traditional melody
arranged by WILLIAM LLEWELLYN

SOLO or SEMI-CHORUS*

*The organ accompaniment may be hummed by the other voices;
use the small notes in bars 31–5, ending at the words 'did say.'

3. God bless his ser-vants in this place That lov-ing-ly do meet; And ma-ny hap-py Christ-mas-es To stran-gers in the street. God bless our ge-ne-ra-tion, Who live both far and near, And we wish them a hap-py, a hap-py New Year, a hap-py New Year!

New Year, New Year!

13. DING-DONG, DING

Words by
G. R. WOODWARD

Melody *O quam mundum, quam
jucundum* from *Piae Cantiones*
harmonized by G. R. WOODWARD

14. DE VIRGIN MARY HAD A BABY BOY

Words traditional

West Indian spiritual
arranged by WILLIAM LLEWELLYN

*The orchestral accompaniment provides a 2-bar introduction.

Melody and words from *The Edric Connor Collection of West Indian Spirituals and Folk Tunes* by permission of Boosey and Hawkes Music Publishers Ltd.

15. DING DONG! MERRILY ON HIGH (i)

Words by
G. R. WOODWARD

French 16th century tune
arranged by WILLIAM LLEWELLYN

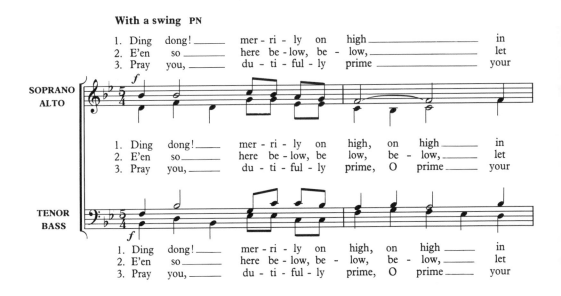

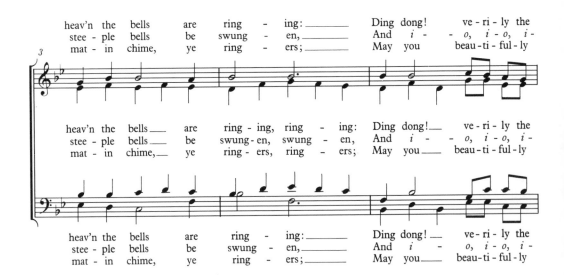

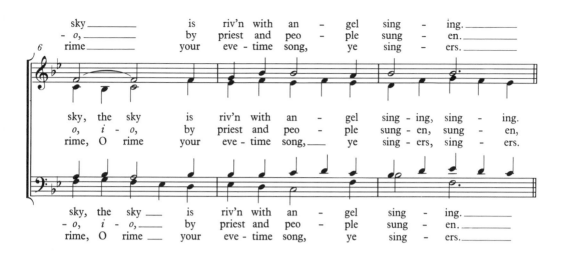

16. DING DONG! MERRILY ON HIGH (ii)

Words by
G.R. WOODWARD

French 16th century tune
arranged by H. LE FEVRE POPE

1. Ding-dong! mer-ri-ly on high, in heav'n the bells are ring-ing:
Ding-dong! ve-ri-ly the sky is riv'n with an-gel sing-ing.

Ding-dong-ding, ding-dong-ding, ding - dong, ding-dong, ding - dong,

Glo - - - - - - -

ding - dong, ding - dong, ding - dong, ding - dong,

- - ri-a, Ho-san-na in ex-cel-sis,_____ ding-dong.

ding - dong, ding - dong, ding-dong-ding-dong, ding-dong.

2. E'en so here below, below,
let steeple bells be swungen,
And *io, io, io,*
by priest and people sungen,

3. Pray you, dutifully prime
your **mattin** chime, ye ringers;
May you beautifully rime
your evetime song, ye singers.

17. DONKEY PLOD AND MARY RIDE

Words by
TIMOTHY DUDLEY-SMITH

ERIC H. THIMAN
arranged by WILLIAM LLEWELLYN

1. Don-key plod and Ma - ry ride, wea - ry Jo - seph walk be-side, theirs the way that all — men come, dark — the night and far — from home — *down the years re-* - mem - ber them, come — a-way, — come — a-way, — come — a-way — to Beth - le-hem.

Melody by Eric Thiman from *The Path to the Moon* by permission of Boosey and Hawkes Music Publishers Ltd.

Words (world excluding USA) © 1976 Timothy Dudley-Smith, (USA) © 1984 Hope Publishing Co., Carol Stream, Ill. 60188.

Arrangement © Copyright 1986 Novello & Company Limited

Reproduced by permission

God on high'. Theirs the song that sounds— a - broad, 'Born— a Sa - viour.

Christ— the Lord'—   down the years re - mem - ber them,

come— a - way,— come— a - way,— come— a - way— to Beth - le - hem.

18. OUR LADY'S LULLABY (i)

Dormi Jesu

Words anon. 18th century

PHILIP RILEY

19. OUR LADY'S LULLABY (ii)

Dormi Jesu

Words anon. 18th century

RICHARD RODNEY BENNETT

Two Lullabies No. 1

20. HARK! THE HERALD ANGELS SING

Words by
C. WESLEY, T. WHITEFIELD
M. MADAN, and others

From a chorus in MENDELSSOHN'S *Festgesang* (1840)
originally adapted by W. H. CUMMINGS
Introduction and arrangement
of last verse by WILLIAM LLEWELLYN

1. Hark! the her - ald an - gels sing ___ Glo - ry to the new - born King;
2. Christ, by high - est heaven a - dored, ___ Christ, the ev - er - last - ing Lord,

Peace on earth and mer - cy mild, ___ God and sin - ners re - con - ciled:
Late in time be - hold him come ___ Off - spring of a Vir - gin's womb!

Joy - ful all ye na - tions rise, ___ Join the tri - umph of the skies, ___
Veiled in flesh the God - head see, ___ Hail the in - car - nate De - i - ty! ___

21. A FANFARE FOR CHRISTMAS

Hodie, hodie

Vespers for Christmas Day

ROBIN WELLS

This Fanfare may be used as an introduction immediately preceding a hymn.

*Bars A and B are alternatives for use as appropriate to the succeeding key.

22. GOD REST YOU MERRY, GENTLEMEN

Words traditional

Traditional London tune
arranged by WILLIAM LLEWELLYN

23. HOW SOFT, UPON THE EV'NING AIR

Words by
IRENE GASS

THOMAS F. DUNHILL
arranged by WILLIAM LLEWELLYN

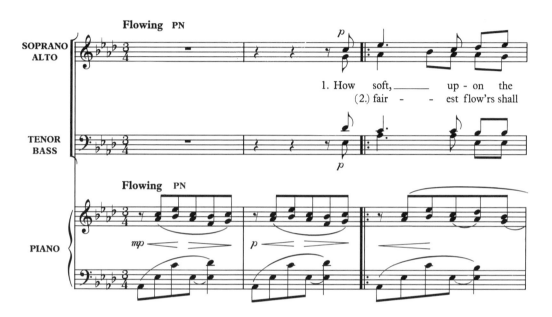

1. How soft,____ up - on the
(2.) fair - - est flow'rs shall

ev - 'ning air There____ seems____ to ech - o still____ The
deck His brow, Their____ fra - grance scent His days,____ While

Arranged and reprinted by permission of the copyright holder and William Elkin Music Services (UK distributors)

for Philip Colls

24. SLUMBER SONG OF THE MADONNA

Hushaby low

Words by
ALFRED NOYES

RONALD FINCH

25. HUSH YOU, MY BABY

Words by
TIMOTHY DUDLEY-SMITH

WILLIAM LLEWELLYN

26 moon - light on moun - tains a - lone, toil - ing and travel - ling so

31 sleep while you can, till the Lord of all glo - ry is seen as a man.

37 S.1.
S.2.
3. Hush you, my ba - by, the years will not stay; the cross on the
A.1.
A.2.

42 hill - top the end of the way. Dim through the dark - ness, in

47 pp
grief and in gloom, the Lord of all glo - ry lies cold in the tomb.
pp

53 T.1.
T.2.
4. Hush you, my ba - by, the Fa - ther on high in power and do -
B.1.
B.2.

26. TROC-A-TRON

I'm a-ridin' to Bethlehem

English words by
JAMES WOODHOUSE

Czech tune arranged
by PETR EBEN

Words reproduced by permission of the Author

Arrangement by Petr Eben reproduced by permission of Möseler Verlag, Wolfenbüttel and Zürich

27. IN DULCI JUBILO

Words translated from
the German source of 1570
by R. L. PEARSALL

Old German melody
set by R. L. PEARSALL
arranged for four voices
by W. J. WESTBROOK

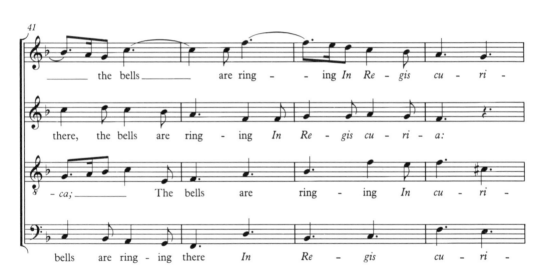

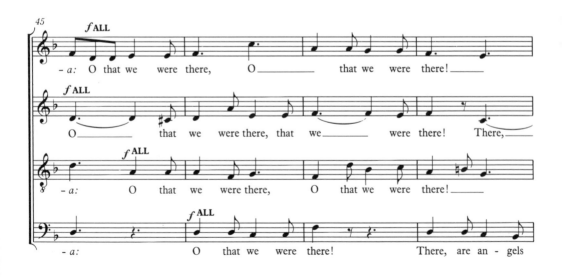

for the Capilla Classica Polifonica of Barcelona

28a. THE SONG OF THE BIRDS

In this most joyful night

English words by
JAMES WOODHOUSE

Traditional Catalan carol
arranged by ENRIQUE RIBO

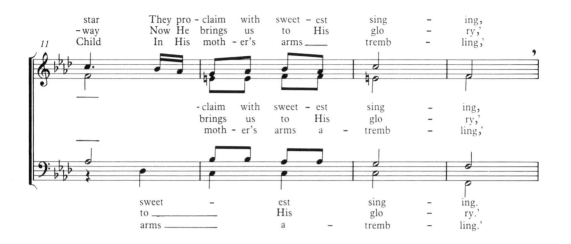

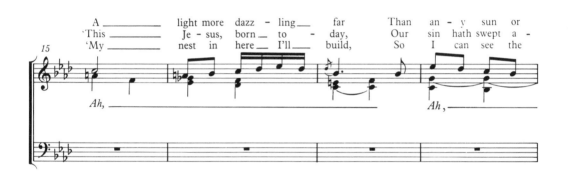

for the Capilla Classica Polifonica of Barcelona

28b. EL CANT DES OCELLS

En veure despuntar

For version with English words
see p.72

Traditional Catalan carol
arranged by ENRIQUE RIBO

Arrangement reproduced by permission of the Composer

for Mildred

29. IN THE BLEAK MID-WINTER (i)

Words by
CHRISTINA GEORGINA ROSSETTI

WILLIAM LLEWELLYN

1. In the bleak mid-win-ter Frost-y wind made moan,

Earth stood hard as i-ron, Wa-ter like a stone; Snow had fall-en,

Wa-ter like a stone;

snow on snow, Snow on snow, In the bleak mid-win-ter, Long a-

Snow on snow, In the

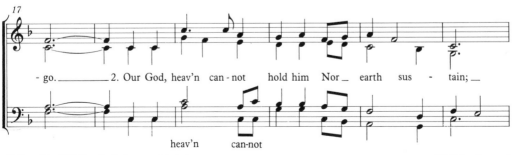

-go. 2. Our God, heav'n can-not hold him Nor earth sus-tain;

heav'n can-not

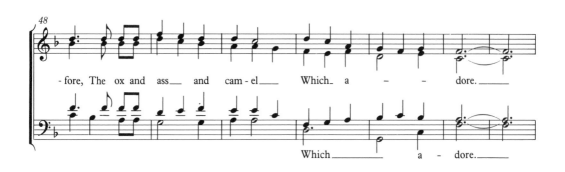

-fore, The ox and ass__ and cam-el__ Which_ a - - dore.__

Which_____ a - dore.__

Firmly

4. An - gels and arch - an - gels May have ga-thered there,_ Che - ru-bim and se - ra-phim_

cresc.

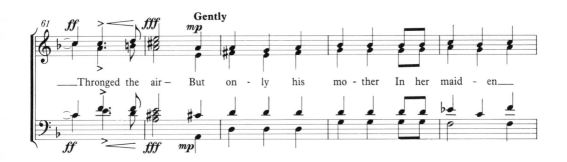

Gently

__Throngèd the air— But on - ly his mo - ther In her maid - en__

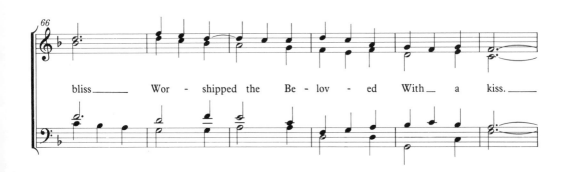

bliss__ Wor - shipped the Be - lov - ed With_ a kiss.__

30. IN THE BLEAK MID-WINTER (ii)

Words by
CHRISTINA GEORGINA ROSETTI

GUSTAV HOLST

31. NINNA-NANNA A GESÙ BAMBINO

In thy mother's arms

English words by
JAMES WOODHOUSE

D. LAVINIO VIRGILI

Words reproduced by permission of the Author

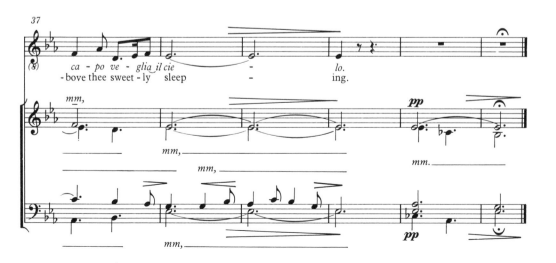

for the Linden Singers

32. I SAW THREE SHIPS (i)

Words traditional

English carol
arranged by IAN HUMPHRIS

33. I SAW THREE SHIPS (ii)

Words traditional

Two English tunes
arranged by WILLIAM LLEWELLYN

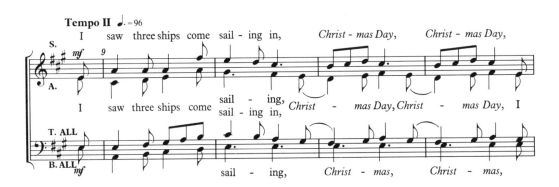

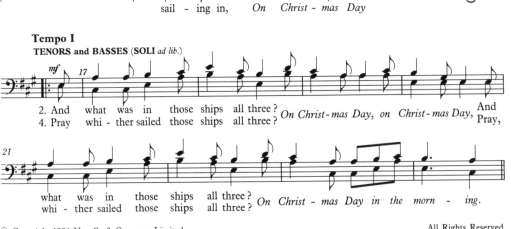

all the an-gels in heav'n_ shall sing,_ On Christ-mas Day in the morn - ing,_ on

On   Christ - mas Day,   on Christ- mas Day in the

Christ - mas Day in the

Fast ♩.=132

ff

Christ - mas, the morn - ing. 8.Then let us all re - joice a-main! *On Christ-mas Day, On*

morn - ing, on Christ-mas Day. *ff*

Slower

Christ-mas Day,Then let us all re - joice a-main! On Christ-mas Day in the morn - - -

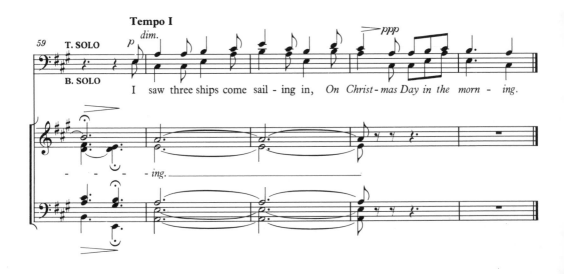

Tempo I

p   dim.   ≥*ppp*

T. SOLO

B. SOLO

I saw three ships come sail - ing in, *On Christ-mas Day in the morn - ing.*

- - - - ing._____

34. I SING OF A MAIDEN

Words traditional
15th century

ROBIN WELLS

Freely PN
SOLO (any voice)

1. I sing of a maid-en That is make-less; King of all kings To her son she ches.*

Andante
S.
A.

2. He came all so still____ Where his mo-ther was,____ As dew in
3. came all so still____ To his mo-ther's bower,____ As dew in
4. came all so still____ Where his mo-ther lay,____ As dew in

T.
B.

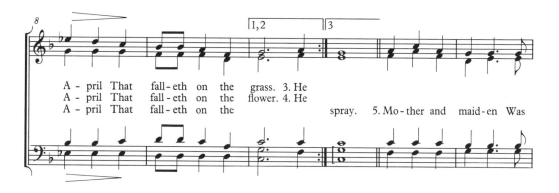

A-pril That fall-eth on the grass. 3. He
A-pril That fall-eth on the flower. 4. He
A-pril That fall-eth on the spray. 5. Mo-ther and maid-en Was

nev-er none but she: Well may such a la-dy God's mo-ther be.

* chose: pronounce 'chezz'

for the Choir of King's College, Cambridge

35. ILLUMINARE, JERUSALEM

Jerusalem rejos for joy

Words anon. 15th century
Bannatyne MS *f.*27v

JUDITH WEIR

to thee are cu-min with lus - ty rout.___ All drest with dy - a -

- man-tis, re - verst with gold in ev - 'ry hem,___ sound-ing at-tone-is[1]___ with a

shou-t: Il - lu-min - a - re,   Je - ru - sa - lem.

Mysterious and urgent

[1] at once, all together

a tempo: strong and deliberate (but not too slow)

The rege- and tir-rant that in_ thee rang, He- rod,_

He-rod, is ex- ile- it

He-rod, is ex- ile- it

The land of Ju –da that jo - sit[1] wrang,_ and

and his off - spring, The land of Ju – da that jo - sit[1] wrang,_ and

and his off - spring, The land of Ju – da that jo - sit[1] wrang,_

when

riss-in is now thy richt-ous king._ So he_ so mych-tie is_ and digne,[2]_ when

riss-in is now thy richt-ous king. So he_ so mych-tie is_ and digne,[2]_ when

he so mych-tie is and digne,[2]_ when

[1] held, harboured [2] worthy

36. JESUS, JESUS, REST YOUR HEAD

Words traditional

Appalachian carol
arranged by ARTHUR WARRELL

37. JOY TO THE WORLD (i)

Words by ISAAC WATTS
based on Psalm 98

mostly from Holford's *Voce di Melodia* (c.1834)
(with echoes of G.F. HANDEL?)

Allegro

SOPRANO
ALTO

1. Joy to the world, the Lord is come! Let earth re - ceive her
2. Joy to the world, the Sa - viour reigns! Let all their songs em -
3. He rules the world with truth and grace, And makes the na - tions

TENOR
BASS

King; Let eve - ry heart pre - pare him room,
- ploy; While fields and floods, rocks, hills and plains
prove The glo - ries of his right - eous - ness

Small notes organ only

And heav'n and na - ture sing, And heav'n and na - ture sing, And
Re - peat the sound-ing joy, Re - peat the sound-ing joy, Re -
And won - ders of his love, And won - ders of his love, And

And heav'n and na - ture sing, And heav'n and na - ture
Re - peat the sound-ing joy, Re - peat the sound-ing
And won - ders of his love, And won - ders of his

heav'n, and heav'n and na - ture sing.
- peat, re - peat the sound - ing joy.
won - ders, won - ders of his love.

sing,
joy,
love,

38. JOY TO THE WORLD (ii)

Words by ISAAC WATTS
based on Psalm 98

mostly from Holford's *Voce di Melodia* (*c.*1834)
(with echoes of G.F. HANDEL?)
arranged by WILLIAM LLEWELLYN

for the Middlesex Federation of Women's Institutes

39. KING JESUS HATH A GARDEN

English words by
G. R. WOODWARD

Dutch carol
arranged by WILLIAM LLEWELLYN

2. The (3.) bon-ny Da-mask-rose is known as Pa - ti - ence:* The
3. The (4.) Crown Im-per-ial bloom-eth too in yon - der place: 'Tis

blithe and thrift-y Ma-ry-gold, O - be - di - ence. *There naught is heard But*
Cha-ri-ty, of stock di-vine, the flower of grace.

Pa-ra-dise bird, Harp, dul-ci-mer, lute, With cym - bal, ___ Trump and tym-bal, And the ten-der,

sooth-ing flute; With cym - bal, ___ Trump and tym-bal, And the ten-der, sooth-ing flute.

* pronounce 'Pay-see-ence'

4. The
5. Yet, 'mid the brave, the brav-est prize of all may claim The

Star of Beth-lem, Je-sus, bles-sed be His Name! *There naught is heard But Pa-ra-dise bird, Harp,*

dul-ci-mer, lute, With cym - bal,___ Trump and tym-bal, And the ten - der, sooth-ing flute; With

cym - bal,___ Trump and tym-bal, And the ten - der, sooth-ing flute.

6. Ah! Je-su Lord, my heal and weal, my bliss com - plete, Make thou my heart thy garden plot, fair, trim and neat, *That I may hear this mu-sick clear: Harp, dul-ci-mer, lute, With cym - bal, —— Trump and tym-bal, And the ten-der, sooth-ing flute; With cym - bal, —— Trump and tym-bal, And the ten-der, sooth-ing flute.* Mm. ——

for the Dean, Organist, and Choir of Canterbury Cathedral

40. OUR LADY AND CHILD

Lady, I sing to thee

Words by
VICTOR DE WAAL

PHILIP MOORE

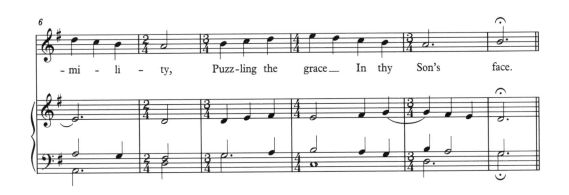

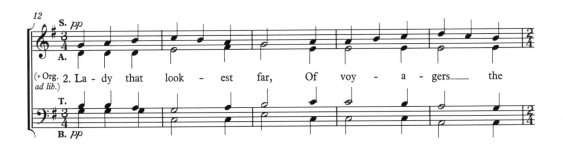

41. LULLAY MY LIKING

Words 15th century

GUSTAV HOLST

Words reproduced from *A Medieval Anthology* (Longman)

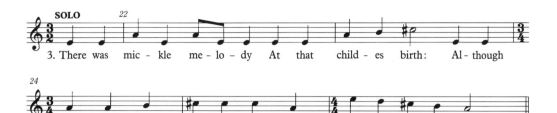

3. There was mic-kle me-lo-dy At that child-es birth: Al-though

they were in hea-ven's bliss They ma-de mic-kle mirth:

REFRAIN

Lul-lay my lik-ing, my dear son, my sweet-ing;

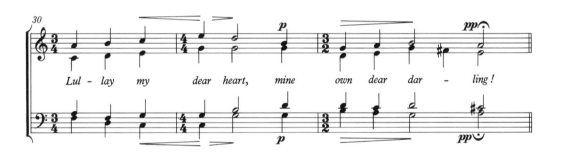

Lul-lay my dear heart, mine own dear dar-ling!

ALL

4. An-gels bright they sang that night And said-en to that child 'Bless-ed be

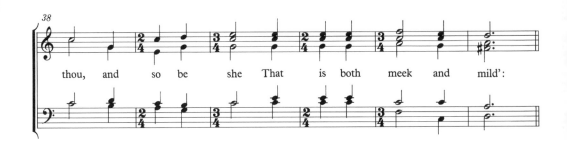

thou,   and   so   be   she   That   is   both   meek   and   mild':

44 REFRAIN

Lul - lay   my   lik - ing,   my   dear   son,   my   sweet - ing;

Lul - lay   my   dear   heart,   mine   own   dear   dar   -   ling!

50 SOLO

5. Pray   we   now   to   that   child,   And   to   his   mo - ther   dear,   God

grant   them   all   his   bless - ing   That   now   mak - en   cheer:

42. COVENTRY CAROL (i)

Lully, lulla, thou little tiny child

Words 15th century
from the Coventry Pageant of the Shearmen and Tailors

KENNETH LEIGHTON
Opus 25

No. 2 of *Three Carols* Opus 25

for the Linden Singers

43. COVENTRY CAROL (ii)

Lully, lulla, thou little tiny child

Words 15th century
from the Coventry Pageant of the Shearmen and Tailors

Modern version of 16th century English tune
by MARTIN SHAW
arranged by IAN HUMPHRIS

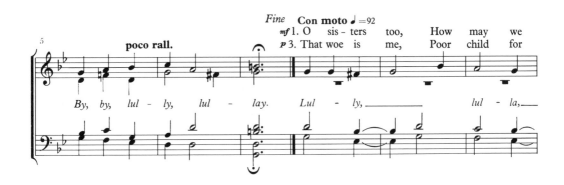

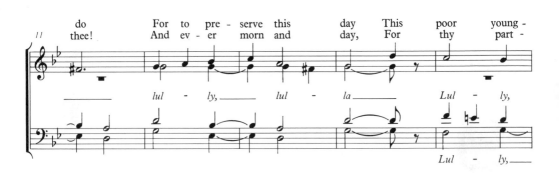

Melody reproduced by permission of A.R. Mowbray and Company Ltd.
Arrangement reproduced by permission of Chandos Records Ltd.

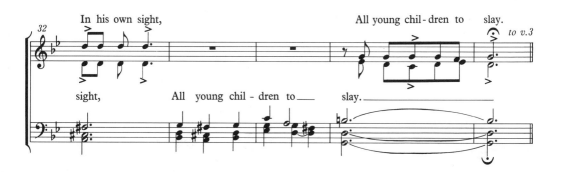

44a. SANT JOSEP I LA MARE DE DEU

Mary, Mother of God's dear child

English words by
JAMES WOODHOUSE

Traditional Catalan carol
arranged by PERE JORDA

1. Mar-y, Mother of God's dear child, __ with Saint Jo-seph made a
day __ they tra - vel far. __ In the evening, faint and
found no lodg - ing there, __ Far too poor they seem for
Joseph finds wood for a fire, Though the wood is far to

SOPRANO ALTO

♩.=84 PN

Oh! _____ oh! oh!
Don!
Oh!

TENOR BASS

Oh! _____ oh! _____

jour-ney. __ 'Twas from Na - za-reth they came; __ It was as the sun was
wear-y __ They seek rest in Beth - le - hem; __ But all folk their doors are
pi - ty. __ They must seek a shel - ter mean __ All of reeds and rush - es
car-ry. __ In the cave, so dark, so cold, __ Je - sus Christ is born to

5

(1.) as the sun was
(2.) all their doors are
(3.) all of rush - es
(4.) Christ is born to

(1.) sun was
(2.) doors are
(3.) rush-es
(4.) born to

oh! _____

oh!

ris - ing.
clos - ing.
wov - en.
Ma - ry.

9

1,2,3. Ma-ry is sing-ing her ba-by to sleep.

4. mf 2. All the
pp 3. They have
ff 4. Now Saint

ba - by to sleep. __ sleep. __

ris - ing.
clos - ing. Don-do-ron - don
wov - en.
Ma - ry.

sing-ing her ba-by to sleep. __

sleep. __

ba - by to sleep. __

44b. SANT JOSEP I LA MARE DE DEU

For version with English words
see p.118

Traditional Catalan carol
arranged by PERE JORDA

45. ROCKING CAROL

Mary's Child, so new and fair

Words by
JAMES WOODHOUSE

Czech carol melody
arranged by WILLIAM LLEWELLYN

* See Performance Notes

46. MARY WALKED THROUGH A WOOD OF THORN

Old German words
translated by E. HERBORN

PHILIP RADCLIFFE

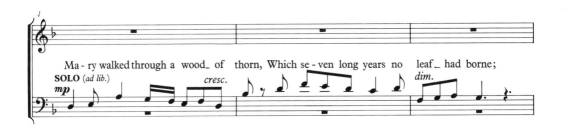

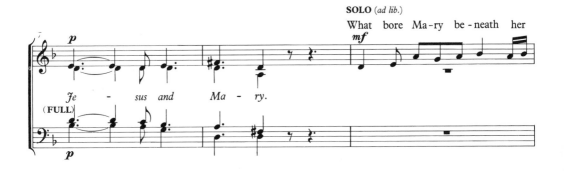

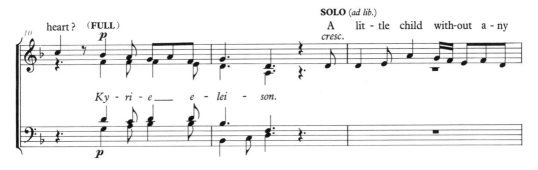

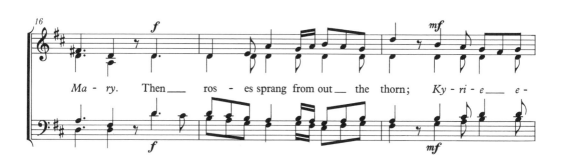

for the choir of St. Peter ad Vincula, H.M. Tower of London

47. NOËL NOUVELET (i)

Noel Nouvelet

English words by
MARION JACKSON

Traditional French carol
arranged by STEPHEN JACKSON

* Bett-lay-emm

* pronounce 's' in 'tous'

4. Bien - tôt les rois, par l'é-toile é - clair-cis, De l'O-
4. Soon the three wise men, who by a star were led, Jour-neyed from the

-rient dont ils é - taient sor - tis, A Beth-lé - em vin-rent un ma-ti-
East, and at the low-ly bed Each bowed the knee and made an of-fer-

* 'st' not pronounced

(1.) No-ël nou-ve-let, No-ël chant-ons i - ci.   Dé - vo-tes gens, cri-ons à Dieu mer-ci!
(1.) 'No-el Nou-ve-let', we sing a new-born King   With our earth-ly song the firm-a-ment shall ring.

Chant-ons No-ël pour le roi nou-ve-let.   No-ël nou-ve-let, No-ël chant-ons i - ci.
See how the love of God such joy doth bring: 'No-el Nou-ve-let' for Christ the new-born King.

for Ashtead Choral Society

48. ALL AND SOME (i)

Nowell sing we

Words 15th century

JEREMY THURLOW

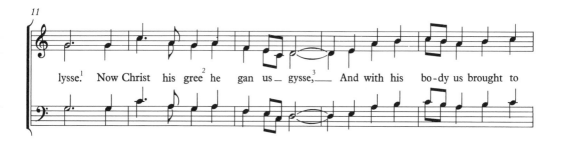

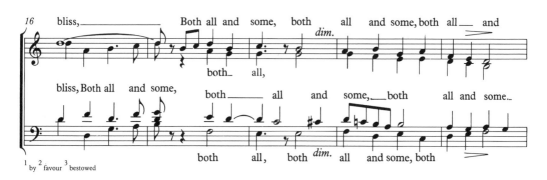

1 by 2 favour 3 bestowed

¹ pitched ² guide ³ tenure

for the Linden Singers

49. NOËL NOUVELET (ii)

Noel, sing Noel

English words by
JAMES WOODHOUSE

Traditional French carol
arranged by IAN HUMPHRIS

With rhythm PN
SOPRANO or TENOR SOLO

1. No-ël nou-ve-let, No-ël chant-ons i - ci; Dé - vo-tes gens, cri -
1. No-el, sing No-el, Good peo-ple sing with glee. Thanks to God on high Who

- ons a Dieu mer - ci. Chant-ons No - ël pour le Roi nou-ve - let, No-ël nou-ve-
set-teth all men free. No - el No - el Let all the na-tions sing, No-el, sing No-

- let, No - ël chant-ons i - ci.
- el To greet the new-born King.

T.

B. La, la-la La, la-la La, la-la La, la-la

S.

2. D'un oi - se - let a - près le chant ou - is. Qui, aux pas-
2. Shep-herds in the field, A small bird sang to them, 'Where's your new-born
4. L'é - toile y vis, qui la nuit é - clair-cit, Qui, d'O - ri -
4. See the East-ern Kings To Beth - l'em make their way; One bright star to

T.

B. La, la-la La, la-la La, la-la La, la-la La, la-la

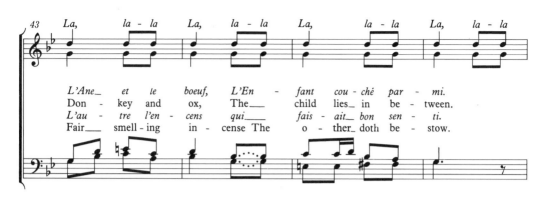

L'Ane__ et le boeuf, L'En - fant cou-ché par - mi.
Don - key and ox, The__ child lies__ in be - tween.
L'au - tre l'en - cens qui__ fais - ait__ bon sen - ti.
Fair__ smell-ing in - cense The o - ther__ doth be - stow.

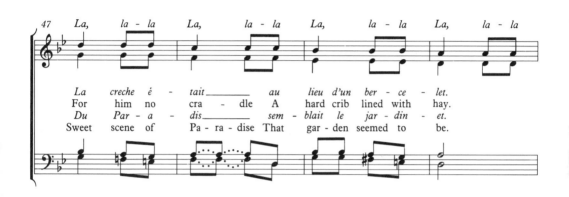

La creche é - tait_____ au lieu d'un ber - ce - let.
For him no cra - dle A hard crib lined with hay.
Du Par - a - dis_____ sem - blait le jar - din - et.
Sweet scene of Pa - ra - dise That gar - den seemed to be.

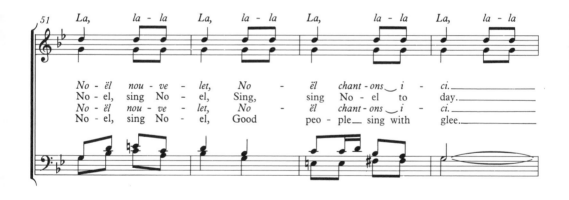

No - ël nou - ve - let, No - ël chant - ons i - ci._____
No - el, sing No - el, Sing, sing No - el to day._____
No - ël nou - ve - let, No - ël chant - ons i - ci._____
No - el, sing No - el, Good peo - ple__ sing with glee._____

50. SIR CHRISTEMAS

Nowell, Nowell, Who is there?

Words 15th century

ROBIN WELLS

*all at once

for Cumnor Choral Society

51. ALL AND SOME (ii)

Nowell sing we

Words 15th century

JOHN BYRT

¹ by ² favour ³ bestowed

¹ misery ² enforce

*The humming can be with open or closed lips, according to the balance of the voices.

out of dis-ease he did__ us dight:__ Both all__ and some, both all__ and some.

No - well sing we, _____ No - well sing

Puer na - tus to us __ was sent, To bliss us bought, fro bale[1] us blent,[2]

we, No - well, _____ No - well, _____

And else to woe we had__ y-went, and else to woe we had__ y-went:

[1] sorrow [2] turned aside

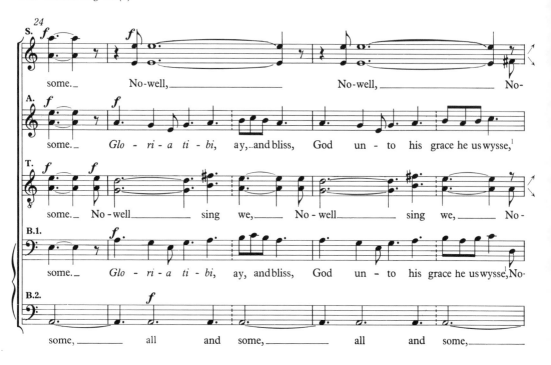

52. ALL AND SOME (iii)

Nowell sing we

Words 15th century
(adapted)

JOHN JOUBERT
Opus 58

* The small notes before the beat

Words from Musica Brittanica Vol. 4 by permission of the Royal Musical Association

simile

53. THE GOLDEN CAROL

Now is Christemas ycome

Words 15th century
(adapted)

PAUL BENDIT

54. SANS DAY CAROL

Now the holly bears a berry

Words traditional

Cornish traditional carol
arranged by IAN HUMPHRIS

SOPRANO: 1. Now the hol - ly bears a ber - ry as white as the milk, And Ma - ry bore Je - sus, who was wrapped up in silk: And Ma - bore Je - sus Christ our Sa - viour for to be, And the first tree in the green-wood, it was the hol - ly, hol - ly, hol - ly! And the first tree in the green-wood, it was the hol - ly!

ALTO: Mm, mm, mm, mm. Mm.

55. ADESTE FIDELES

O come, all ye faithful

Words 18th century
trans. FREDERICK OAKLEY and others

18th century melody probably by J.F. WADE
harmonized mainly by W.H. MONK
Verse 5 arranged by H.A. CHAMBERS
Verse 6 arranged by WILLIAM LLEWELLYN

Maestoso PN

SOPRANO
ALTO

1. O come, all ye faith - ful, Joy - ful and tri - umph - ant, O come ye, O
2. God of___ God,___ Light_ of_ Light,___ Lo! he ab-
3. See how the shep - herds, Summoned to his cra - dle, Leav - ing their
4. Lo! star - led chief - tains, Ma - gi, Christ a - dor - ing, Of - fer him
5. *Sing, choirs of An - gels, Sing in ex - ul - ta - tion, Sing,_ all ye
6. *Yea, Lord, we greet thee, Born this hap - py morn - ing, Je - su to

TENOR
BASS

come __ ye to Beth - le - hem; Come and_ be - hold_ him,
- hors __ not the Vir - gin's womb; Ve - ry ___ God,— Be-
flocks, draw nigh with low - ly fear; We too_ will thi - ther
in - cense,_ gold,___ and myrrh; We to_ the Christ - child
ci - ti - zens of heav'n __ a - bove; Glo - ry_ to God ___
thee __ be ___ glo - ry given; Word of_ the Fa - ther,

Born the King of An - gels:
- got - ten, not cre - a - ted:
Bend our joy - ful foot - steps: O come, let us a - dore him, O come, let us a-
Bring our hearts' o - bla - tions:
In ___ the_ high - est:
Now in flesh ap - pear - ing:

- dore him, O come, let us a - dore him,___ Christ ___ the Lord!

*for extended versions of these verses see pp. 165-167.

for the Inner London Education Authority Central
Young Musicians' Chamber Choir

56. O LEAVE YOUR SHEEP

Traditional French tune
Quittez pasteurs
arranged by IAN HUMPHRIS

English words by
ALICE RALEIGH

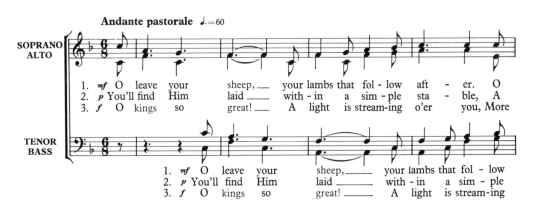

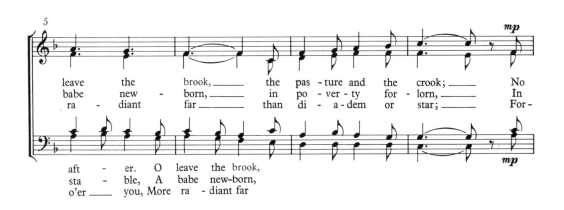

shep - herds seek your goal! _____ Your Lord, _____ your Lord, _____ your
search the world for you: _____ 'Tis He, _____ 'tis He, _____ 'tis
won - der shall be told: _____ Bring myrrh, _____ bring myrrh, _____ bring

Lord who com - eth to _____ con - sole! _____ Your Lord, _____ your
He, 'tis He the shep - herd _____ true! _____ 'Tis He, _____ 'tis
myrrh, bring frank - in - cense _____ and _____ gold! _____ Bring myrrh, _____ bring

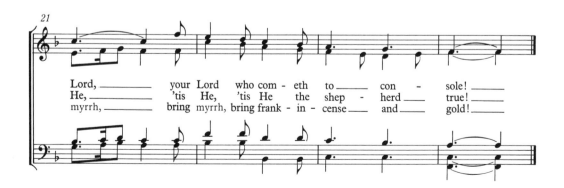

Lord, _____ your Lord who com - eth to _____ con - sole! _____
He, _____ 'tis He, 'tis He the shep - herd _____ true! _____
myrrh, _____ bring myrrh, bring frank - in - cense _____ and _____ gold! _____

57. O MAGNUM MISTERIUM

GIOVANNI GABRIELI
edited by WILLIAM LLEWELLYN

58. BALULALOW (i)

Paraphrase of Luther's
Vom Himmel Hoch in
*Ane Compendious Buik of Godly
and Spiritual Sangis,* 1567

O my dear heart

RICHARD RODNEY BENNETT

59. ONCE IN ROYAL DAVID'S CITY

Words by
CECIL FRANCES ALEXANDER

HENRY J. GAUNTLETT
arranged by A. H. MANN
last verse arranged by ROBIN WELLS

60. BALULALOW (ii)

O my dear heart

Paraphrase of Luther's
Vom Himmel Hoch in
*Ane Compendions Buik of
Godly and Spiritual Sangis*, 1567
adapted by ANTHONY PETTI

PAUL JOHNSON

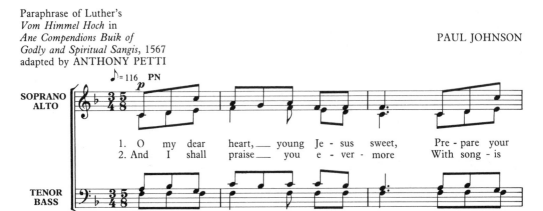

1. O my dear heart, young Je - sus sweet, Pre - pare your
2. And I shall praise you e - ver - more With song - is

cra - dle in my spreit, And I shall rock you in my
sweet un - to your gloir; With all my heart to you I

bow, And ne - ver - more from you de - part.
And sing that richt Ba - lu - la - low.

Reprinted from *The New Catholic Hymnal* by permission of the publishers Faber Music Limited and Paul Johnson

61. THE TWELVE DAYS OF CHRISTMAS

On the First day of Christmas

Words traditional

Traditional English tune
with additions by FREDERIC AUSTIN
arranged by IAN HUMPHRIS

62. LONDON WAITS (i)

Past three o'clock

Words by
G. R. WOODWARD
with traditional refrain

Tune *London Waits*
harmonized by
CHARLES WOOD

Past three o' clock, And a cold __ frost-y morn-ing; Past three o'__

clock; Good __ mor-row, mas-ters all! Born is a Ba - by, Gen-tle as

may be, Son __ of __ th' e - ter - nal Fa - ther su - per - nal.

2. Seraph quire singeth,
Angel bell ringeth:
Hark how they rime it,
Time it, and chime it.

3. Mid earth rejoices
Hearing such voices
Ne'ertofore so well
Carolling *Nowell*.

4. Hinds o'er the pearly
Dewy lawn early
Seek the high stranger
Laid in the manger.

5. Cheese from the dairy
Bring they for Mary,
And, not for money,
Butter and honey.

6. Light out of star-land
Leadeth from far land
Princes, to meet him,
Worship and greet him.

7. Myrrh from full coffer,
Incense they offer:
Nor is the golden
Nugget withholden.

8. Thus they: I pray you,
Up, sirs, nor stay you
Till ye confess him
Likewise, and bless him.

63. LONDON WAITS (ii)

Past three o'clock

Words by
G. R. WOODWARD
with traditional refrain

Quodlibet
arranged by WILLIAM LLEWELLYN

64. A GALLERY CAROL

Rejoice and be merry

Words traditional

Old English tune
arranged by ROBIN WELLS

1. Re-joice and be mer-ry in songs and in mirth, O praise our Re-deem-er, all mor-tals on earth. For this is the birth-day of Je-sus our King, Who brought us sal-va-tion, his prais-es we'll sing.

3. Like-wise a bright star in the sky did ap-pear, ___ Which led the Wise Men from the east to draw near; They found the Mes-si-ah, sweet Je-sus our King, Who ___ brought us sal-va-tion, his prais-es we'll sing.

for Gerald Smith and the Choir of St. Dominic's

65. REJOICE LORDINGS

Words Early English

ARTHUR OLDHAM

bore   a   child   with - out - en   sin,

Keep   us   all   from   hel - le   pin!   De

vir - gi - ne Ma - ri - a.

66. IL EST NÉ, LE DIVIN ENFANT

See him born, the Heavenly Child

English words by
JAMES WOODHOUSE

French traditional carol
arranged by WILLIAM LLEWELLYN

67. A CHRISTMAS ANTIPHON (i)

See, to us a child is born

A Christmas Antiphon
based on Isaiah 9.6,7
TIMOTHY DUDLEY-SMITH

Tune *Lauds*
JOHN WILSON

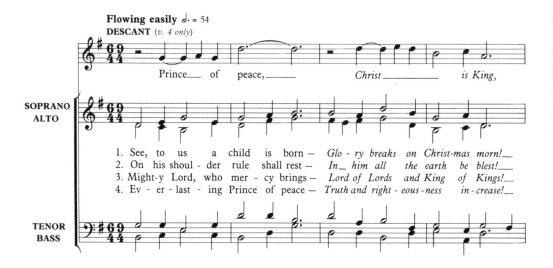

Prince of peace, Christ is King,

1. See, to us a child is born — *Glo - ry breaks on Christ-mas morn!*
2. On his shoul - der rule shall rest — *In him all the earth be blest!*
3. Might-y Lord, who mer - cy brings — *Lord of Lords and King of Kings!*
4. Ev - er - last - ing Prince of peace — *Truth and right - eous-ness in - crease!*

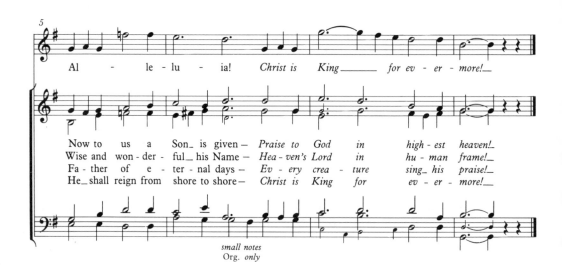

Al - le - lu - ia! *Christ is King for ev - er - more!*

Now to us a Son is given — *Praise to God in high - est heaven!*
Wise and won - der - ful his Name — *Hea - ven's Lord in hu - man frame!*
Fa - ther of e - ter - nal days — *Ev - ery crea - ture sing his praise!*
He shall reign from shore to shore — *Christ is King for ev - er - more!*

small notes
Org. only

68. A CHRISTMAS ANTIPHON (ii)

See, to us a child is born

A Christmas Antiphon
based on Isaiah 9.6,7 by
TIMOTHY DUDLEY-SMITH

Tune *Lauds* by JOHN WILSON
arranged by WILLIAM LLEWELLYN

Music (*Lauds*) reproduced by permission of Oxford University Press
Words (world excluding USA) © 1976 Timothy Dudley-Smith
Words (USA) © 1983 by Hope Publishing Co., Carol Stream, Ill. 60188. Reproduced by permission

69. STILLE NACHT

Silent night

German words by JOSEPH MOHR
English words adapted by JAMES WOODHOUSE

Melody by FRANZ GRÜBER
arranged by IAN HUMPHRIS

70. THE INFANT KING

Sing lullaby!

Words by
S. BARING-GOULD

Traditional Basque Noël
arranged by WILLIAM LLEWELLYN

for Ashtead Choral Society

71. LUTE-BOOK LULLABY

Sweet was the song the Virgin sang

Words from the Lute-Book of
WILLIAM BALLET (17th cent.)

Jeremy Thurlow

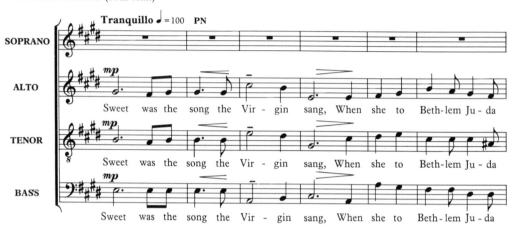

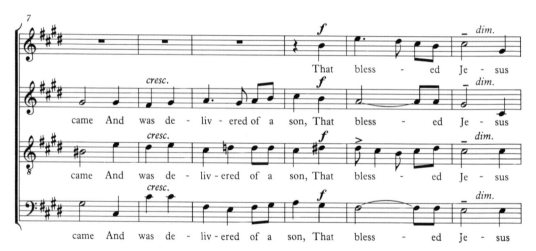

72. GABRIEL'S MESSAGE

The angel Gabriel from heaven came

Words by
S. BARING-GOULD

Basque carol
arranged by WILLIAM LLEWELLYN

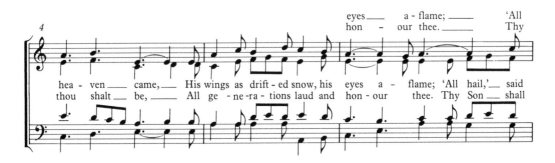

*Omit if unaccompanied.

Melody © 1961 H. Freeman & Co. Reproduced by permission of EMI Music Publishing Ltd and International Music Publications

* Omit if unaccompanied

73. CAROL OF THE CHRIST-CHILD

The Christ-child lay on Mary's lap

Words by
G. K. CHESTERTON

PHILIP RILEY

1. The Christ-child lay on Ma - ry's lap, His hair was like __ a

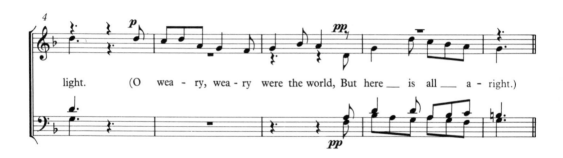

light. (O wea - ry, wea - ry were the world, But here __ is all __ a - right.)

2. The Christ - child lay on Ma - ry's breast, His _ hair _ was like _ a

star. (O stern_ and cun - ning are the Kings, But here the true_ hearts are.)

74. THE FIRST NOWELL

Traditional English carol
arranged by JOHN STAINER
descant and final verse
arranged by WILLIAM LLEWELLYN

Words traditional

1. The First Nowell the angel did say Was to certain poor
2. They looked up and saw a star Shining in the
3. And by the light of that same star, Three Wise Men

shep-herds in fields as they lay; In fields where they lay, keep-ing their
east, be-yond them far; And to the earth it gave great
came from coun-try far; To seek for a King was their in-

DESCANT

No - well, No -

sheep, On a cold win-ter's night that was so deep:
light, And so it con-tin-ued both day and night: No - well, No -
-tent, And to fol-low the star where-ev-er it went:

for verses 4 – 6 see p.230

- well, No - well, No - well, No - well, No - well, No - well, No - well.

- well, No - well, No - well, Born is the King of Is - ra - el.

This layout makes possible the singing of *The First Nowell* interspersed with verses of *Mary's Child* (see Performing Notes).

75. MARY'S CHILD

Born in the night

Words by
GEOFFREY AINGER

GEOFFREY AINGER
arranged by WILLIAM LLEWELLYN

for verses 3 and 4 see p.231

This layout makes possible the singing of *Mary's Child* interspersed with verses of *The First Nowell* (see Performing Notes).

* see page 232 for final verse arrangement

234

76. THE HOLLY AND THE IVY

Words traditional

Gloucestershire Folk Carol
collected by CECIL SHARP
arranged by WILLIAM LLEWELLYN

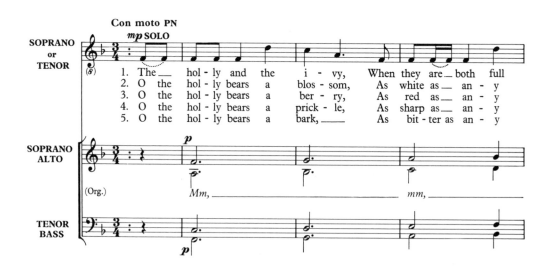

1. The__ hol - ly and the i - vy, When they are__ both full
2. O the hol - ly bears a blos - som, As white as __ an - y
3. O the hol - ly bears a ber - ry, As red as __ an - y
4. O the hol - ly bears a prick - le, As sharp as __ an - y
5. O the hol - ly bears a bark, ____ As bit - ter as an - y

Mm, _____ mm, _____

grown, Of __ all the trees that are in the wood, The__ hol - ly bears the__ crown:
flower, And__ Ma - ry bore sweet__ Je - sus Christ, To __ be our sweet Sav - iour:
blood, And__ Ma - ry bore sweet__ Je - sus Christ To __ do poor sin - ners__ good:
thorn, And__ Ma - ry bore sweet__ Je - sus Christ On __ Christmas Day in the morn:
gall, And__ Ma - ry bore sweet__ Je - sus Christ For __ to re - deem us__ all:

mm, _____ mm. _____

77. THE TREES OF THE FIELD

The oak stands fast

Words by
E. M. JAMESON

DAVID STONE

78. THERE IS NO ROSE OF SUCH VIRTUE

Words Medieval

JOHN JOUBERT

79. THE SHEPHERDS' FAREWELL

Thou must leave thy lowly dwelling

Words by
PAUL ENGLAND

HECTOR BERLIOZ

80. TORCHES! (i)

Words translated
from the Galician
by J. B. TREND

JOHN JOUBERT

Words from *The Oxford Book of Carols* by permission of Oxford University Press

81. TORCHES! (ii)

Words translated
from the Galician
by J. B. TREND

JOHN JOUBERT

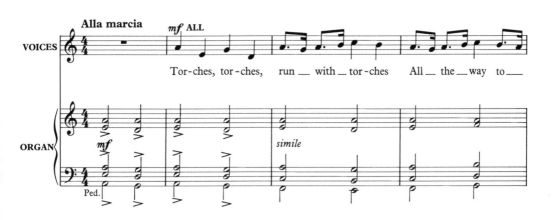

Words from *The Oxford Book of Carols* by permission of Oxford University Press

82. HURON CAROL

'Twas in the moon of wintertime

Attributed to Father JEAN DE BREBEUF
English words by J.E. MIDDLETON

Tune of the Huron Indians
arranged by WILLIAM LLEWELLYN

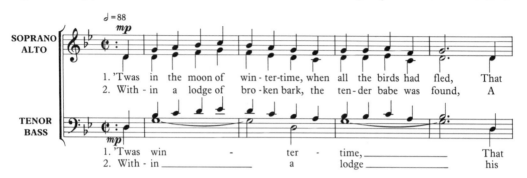

1. 'Twas in the moon of win-ter-time, when all the birds had fled, That
2. With-in a lodge of bro-ken bark, the ten-der babe was found, A

1. 'Twas win - ter - time, _____ That
2. With-in _____ a lodge _____ his

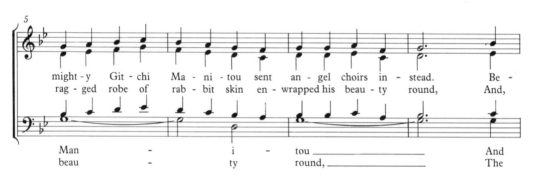

might-y Git-chi Ma - ni - tou sent an - gel choirs in - stead. Be-
rag-ged robe of rab - bit skin en - wrapped his beau - ty round, And,

Man - i - tou _____ And
beau - ty round, _____ The

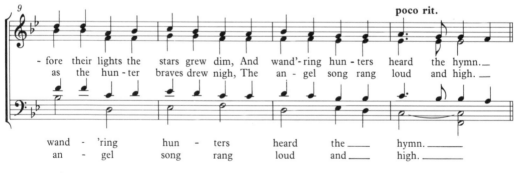

poco rit.

- fore their lights the stars grew dim, And wand'-ring hun - ters heard the hymn._
as the hun - ter braves drew nigh, The an - gel song rang loud and high._

wand - 'ring hun - ters heard the ___ hymn. _____
an - gel song rang loud and ___ high. _____

a tempo

Je - sus your King is born,_ Je - sus is born,_ in ex - cel - sis glo - ri - a.
Je - sus_ your Je - sus is_

Je - sus, Je - sus _____ is born, _____ glo - ri - a.

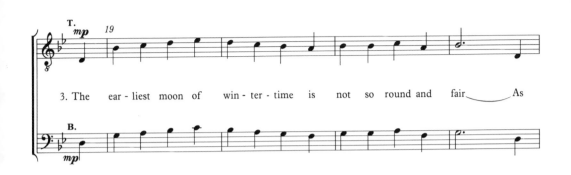

3. The ear-liest moon of win-ter-time is not so round and fair.___ As

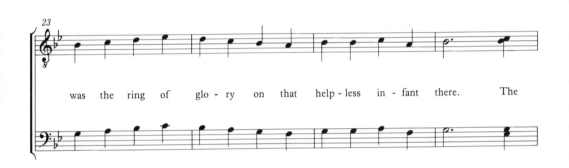

was the ring of glo-ry on that help-less in-fant there. The

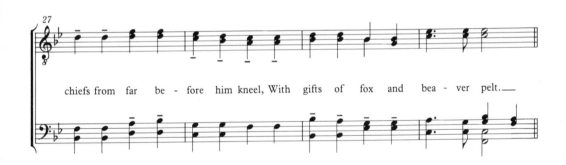

chiefs from far be-fore him kneel, With gifts of fox and bea-ver pelt.___

Je-sus your King is born, Je-sus is born,___ in ex-cel-sis glo-ri - a.

Je-sus___ your King is born,___ Je-sus is___ born,___ in ex-cel-sis glo-ri - a.

Je - sus Je - sus___ is born,___ glo - ri - a.

83. EL NOI DE LA MARE

What shall we give?

English words by
JAMES WOODHOUSE

Traditional Catalan carol
arranged by ENRIQUE RIBO

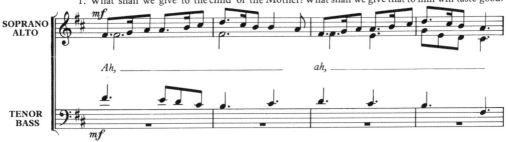

Arrangement reproduced by permission of the Composer

Copyright by Enrique Ribo

English words reproduced by permission of the Author

84. TYRLE, TYRLOW

Words from
Balliol MS 1536

HEALEY WILLAN

shepherds a-non _____ gan them a-spy. _____ Tyr-

-le, tyr-low, tyr-le, tyr-low! *Glo-ri-a in ex-cel-sis,* the an-gels sang, And

said that peace was pre-sent a-mong To ev-'ry man that _____ to the faith_ would

fong.[1] _____ Tyr-le, tyr-low, tyr-le, tyr-low! The

shep-herds hied them to Bed-lem, To see that bless-ed Sun_ His beam; And

there_ they found _____ that glo-rious leme.[2] _____ Tyr-

[1] accept [2] ray

85. PUER NOBIS

Unto us is born a son

English words by
G.R. WOODWARD

Tune: *Piae Cantiones*, 1582
arranged by WILLIAM LLEWELLYN

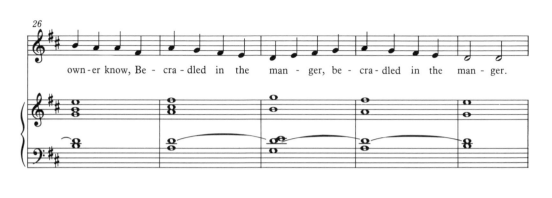

owner know, Be-cra-dled in the man-ger, be-cra-dled in the man-ger.

TENORS and BASSES

3. This did He-rod sore af-fray, And griev-ous-ly be-wil - der, So he gave the

Ped.

word to slay, And slew the lit-tle chil - der, and slew the lit-tle chil - der.

dim.

SOPRANOS

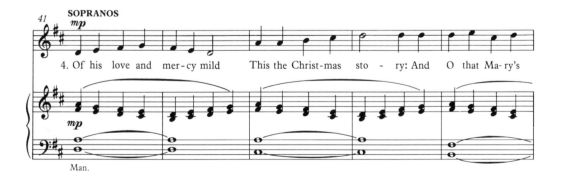

4. Of his love and mer-cy mild This the Christ-mas sto - ry: And O that Ma-ry's

Man.

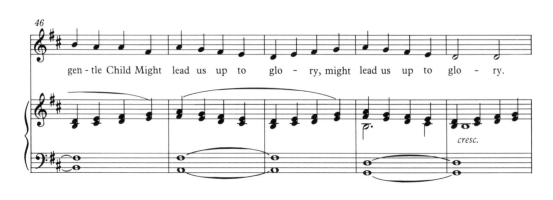

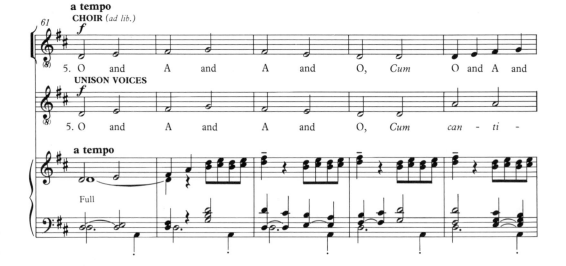

86. JOY SHALL BE YOURS IN THE MORNING

Villagers all, this frosty tide

Words by
KENNETH GRAHAME

H. FRASER-SIMSON

Copyright 1930 by Chappell & Co.

for the Linden Singers

87. THE YORKSHIRE WASSAIL

Wassail: We've been a while a-wandering

Words traditional

Yorkshire carol
arranged by IAN HUMPHRIS

88. CANON FOR THREE CHOIRS

Worship the Christ-child

Words by
WILLIAM LLEWELLYN

W. A. MOZART
K.348

5

born in a sta - ble: Where? Where?
He is our Sav - iour: Here! Here!
sleep in your cra - dle: Sleep! Sleep!

Christ - child, we seek the Christ - child: Where?
ba - by, here is the ba - by: Here!
cra - dle, sleep in your cra - dle: Sleep!

sta - ble: Where? Where? Where? Where?
come to us: Here! Here! Here!
ba - by, Sleep! Sleep! Sleep! Sleep!

Where? The ba - by Je - sus: Where?
Here! Our Sav - iour Je - sus: Here!
Sleep! Sleep in your cra - dle: Sleep!

7   (Choir 3 **rit.** – – – – – – – – – 𝄐)

4. Wor - ship the Christ - child born in a sta - ble.

4. Wor - ship the Christ - child __ born in a sta - ble.

4. Wor - ship the Christ - child __ born in a sta - ble.

4. Wor - ship the Christ - child born in a sta - ble.

89. WHENCE IS THAT GOODLY
FRAGRANCE FLOWING? (i)

English words by
A.B. RAMSAY

French traditional carol
arranged by WILLIAM LLEWELLYN

for Farnham and Bourne Choral Society

90. WHENCE IS THAT GOODLY FRAGRANCE FLOWING? (ii)

English words by
A.B. RAMSAY

French traditional carol
arranged by ROBIN WELLS

1. Whence is that good-ly fra-grance flow-ing, Steal-ing our sen-ses all a - way?
2. What is that light so bril-liant, break-ing Here in the night a-cross our eyes?
3. Beth - le-hem! there in man-ger ly - ing, Find your Re-deem-er, haste a - way,

Ne-ver the like did come a - blow-ing, Shepherds, from flow-'ry fields in May;
Ne-ver so bright, the day-star wak-ing, Start-ed to climb the morn-ing skies!
Run ye with ea-ger foot-steps hie-ing, Wor-ship the Sa-viour born to-day.

Whence is that good-ly fra-grance flow-ing, Steal-ing our sen-ses all a - way?
What is that light so bril-liant, break-ing Here in the night a-cross our eyes?
Beth - le-hem! there in man-ger ly - ing, Find your Re-deem-er, haste a -

- way, Find your Re-deem - er, haste a way.
- way, Find your Re-deem - er, haste a - way.
- way, Find your Re-deem - er, haste a - way.

Words reprinted by permission of the Master and Fellows of Magdelene College, Cambridge

© Copyright 1986 Novello & Company Limited

INDEX

ABBREVIATIONS: U = Unaccompanied S = Soprano A = Alto T = Tenor B = Bass Br = Baritone Perc. = Percussion Tp = Timpani

ORCHESTRAL FORCES: Wind (2222) = 2 Flutes, 2 Oboes, 2 Clarinets, 2 Bassoons; Brass (2231) = 2 Horns, 2 Trumpets, 3 Trombones, 1 Tuba; Tp+2 = Timpani+2 further percussion players

NO.	PAGE	U	TITLE AND FIRST LINE (both are shown)	TIME	COMPOSER OR ARRANGER	Minimum Choir	Solo	Wind	Brass	Perc.	Strings	JUNIOR BOOK (NJBC)
88	270	U	Canon for three choirs (Worship the Christ-child)	1'30"	W. A. Mozart/W. Ll.	[SATB]×3						
73	226	U	Carol of the Christ-child (The Christ-child lay)	1'30"	Philip Riley	SATB						
11	23	U	Christmas Eve (The Oxen)	2'30"	Benjamin Britten	SA						
9	20	U	Christmas is coming	1'40"	Walford Davies	SATB						
12	26		Come all you worthy people here (A Somerset Carol)	1'30"	William Llewellyn	SATB		2222	2231	Tp+2	Strings	NJBC
42	113	U	Coventry Carol (Lully, lulla) (i)	2'30"	Kenneth Leighton	SATBB	S					
43	116	U	Coventry Carol (Lully, lulla) (ii)	2'25"	Ian Humphris	SSAATTBB						
8	18	U	Dawn Carol (Blessed be he that cometh)	3'15"	Malcolm Williamson	SAATTB						
14	30		De Virgin Mary had a baby boy	2'20"	William Llewellyn	TTBB	Br	2222	2231	Tp+2	Strings	NJBC
13	29	U	Ding-dong, ding	1'30"	G. R. Woodward	SATB						
15	34	U	Ding dong! merrily on high (i)	2'10"	William Llewellyn	SATB						
16	36	U	Ding dong! merrily on high (ii)	2'00"	H. Le Fèvre Pope	SSA						
17	37		Donkey plod and Mary ride	4'30"	Eric Thiman/W. Ll.	SATB						
18	43	U	Dormi Jesu (Our Lady's Lullaby) (i)	0'45"	Philip Riley	SSAA						
19	44	U	Dormi Jesu (Our Lady's Lullaby) (ii)	1'30"	Richard R. Bennett	SSAA						
28b	74	U	E1 Cant des Ocells (En veure despuntar)	3'00"	Enrique Ribo	SATB	S					
83	253	U	El Noi de la Mare (What shall we give?)	1'50"	Enrique Ribo	SSAATTBB						
28b	74	U	En veure despuntar (E1 Cant des Ocells)	3'00"	Enrique Ribo	SATB	S					
6	14	U	Fum, fum, fum (Ancient prophets first foretold him)	1'10"	William Llewellyn	SATTB						NJBC
72	223	U	Gabriel's message (The angel Gabriel)	2'15"	William Llewellyn	SATB		1200			Strings	NJBC
22	50		God rest you merry, gentlemen	2'00"	William Llewellyn	SSATBB		2222	2231	Tp+2	Strings	NJBC
20	46		Hark! the herald angels sing	3'20"	Mendelssohn/W. Ll.	SATB		2222	2231	Tp+2	Strings	NJBC
21	49	U	Hodie, hodie (A Fanfare for Christmas)	1'00"	Robin Wells	SATB		2222	2231	Tp+2	Strings	
23	57		How soft, upon the ev'ning air	1'40"	Thomas Dunhill/W. Ll.	SAATTBB		2200			Strings	

82	250	U	Huron Carol ('Twas in the moon of wintertime)	1'50"	William Llewellyn	SSAATTBB					Strings	NJBC
24	60	U	Hushaby low (Slumber Song of the Madonna)	2'00"	Ronald Finch	SAATTBB	S					
25	63	U	Hush you, my baby	3'10"	William Llewellyn	SSAATTBB	ST					
66	209	U	Il est né, le divin enfant (See him born)	2'00"	William Llewellyn	SSAATTBB		1200			Strings	NJBC
35	90	U	Illuminare, Jerusalem (Jerusalem rejos for joy)	2'30"	Judith Weir	SSAATTBB						
26	66	U	I'm a-ridin' to Bethlehem (Troc-a-tron)	0'50"	Petr Eben	SATB						
27	68	U	In dulci jubilo	3'45"	R. L. Pearsall	SATB						
29	76	U	In the bleak mid-winter (i)	3'45"	William Llewellyn	SATB						
30	80	U	In the bleak mid-winter (ii)	3'45"	Gustav Holst	SATB		1111			Strings	NJBC
28a	72	U	In this most joyful night (The Song of the Birds)	3'00"	Enrique Ribo	SATB						
31	81	U	In thy mother's arms (Ninna-Nanna)	1'50"	D. Lavinio Virgili	SATB	A/Br					
32	84	U	I saw three ships (i)	1'00"	Ian Humphris	SATB						
33	86	U	I saw three ships (ii)	2'05"	William Llewellyn	SAATTBB	TB					
34	89	U	I sing of a maiden	1'20"	Robin Wells	SATTB						
35	90		Jerusalem rejos for joy (Illuminare, Jerusalem)	2'30"	Judith Weir	SSAATTBB						
36	95	U	Jesus, Jesus, rest your head	2'20"	J. J. Niles/Warrell	SATB						
86	264	U	Joy shall be yours (Villagers all, this frosty tide)	1'30"	H. Fraser-Simson	SATB						
37	98	U	Joy to the World (i)	1'30"	? G. F. Handel	SATB		2222	2231	Tp	Strings	NJBC
38	99	U	Joy to the World (ii)	2'00"	? G. F. Handel/W. Ll.	SATB		2222	0200	Tp	Strings	
39	104		King Jesus hath a garden	3'05"	William Llewellyn	SSAA		2221	2200	Tp+2	Strings	NJBC
40	108	U	Lady, I sing to thee (Our Lady and Child)	1'40"	Philip Moore	SSATB						
62	195	U	London Waits (Past three o'clock) (i)	2'00"	Charles Wood	SATB						
63	196	U	London Waits (Past three o'clock) (ii)	3'00"	William Llewellyn	SSAATTBB	Br					NJBC
41	110	U	Lullay my liking	2'30"	Gustav Holst	SATB						
42	113	U	Lully, lulla (Coventry Carol) (i)	2'30"	Kenneth Leighton	SATBB	S					
43	116	U	Lully, lulla (Coventry Carol) (ii)	2'25"	Ian Humphris	SSAATTBB						
71	220	U	Lute-book Lullaby (Sweet was the song the Virgin sang)	2'15"	Jeremy Thurlow	SSAATTBB						

NO.	PAGE	U	TITLE AND FIRST LINE (both are shown)	TIME	COMPOSER OR ARRANGER	VOICES Minimum Choir	Solo	INSTRUMENTAL PARTS (on hire) Wind	Brass	Perc.	Strings	JUNIOR BOOK (NJBC)
44a	118	U	*Mary, Mother of God's dear child (Sant Josep i la Mare)*	1'30"	*Père Jorda*	SATB	A/Br					
75	229	U	*Mary's Child (Born in the night)*	1'40"	*Geoffrey Ainger/W. Ll.*	SATTBB						NJBC
45	120	U	*Mary's Child, so new and fair (Rocking Carol)*	1'35"	*William Llewellyn*	SAATTBB						NJBC
46	124	U	*Mary walked through a wood of thorn*	1'05"	*Philip Radcliffe*	SATB						
31	81	U	*Ninna-Nanna (In thy mother's arms)*	1'50"	*D. Lavinio Virgili*	SATB						
47	126	U	*Noel Nouvelet (Noël Nouvelet) (i)*	3'20"	*Stephen Jackson*	SSAATTBB	S	2222	2230	Tp+1	Strings	
49	137	U	*Noël Nouvelet (Noel, sing Noel) (ii)*	2'35"	*Ian Humphris*	SATB						
49	137	U	*Noel, sing Noel (Noël Nouvelet) (ii)*	2'35"	*Ian Humphris*	SATB						
50	140	U	*Nowell, Nowell, Who is there? (Sir Christemas)*	1'05"	*Robin Wells*	SATBB						
48	133	U	*Nowell sing we (All and some) (i)*	1'55"	*Jeremy Thurlow*	SSAATTBB		1111	1111	0+3	Strings	
51	142	U	*Nowell sing we (All and some) (ii)*	3'35"	*John Byrt*	SSAATTBB	S					
52	148	U	*Nowell sing we (All and some) (iii)*	2'40"	*John Joubert*	SATB						
53	156	U	*Now is Christemas ycome (The Golden Carol)*	1'10"	*Paul Bendit*	SSAATTBB						
54	160	U	*Now the holly bears a berry (Sans Day Carol)*	1'50"	*Ian Humphris*	SAATTBB						
55	164	U	*O come, all ye faithful*	4'20"	*William Llewellyn*	SATB		2222	2231	Tp+3	Strings	NJBC
56	168	U	*O leave your sheep*	2'15"	*Ian Humphris*	SATB						
57	170	U	*O magnum misterium*	2'15"	*Giovanni Gabrieli/ W. Ll.*	SATB: TTBB			1210: 1021			
58	183	U	*O my dear heart (Balulalow) (i)*	1'05"	*Richard R. Bennett*	SSSA						
60	186	U	*O my dear heart (Balulalow) (ii)*	1'40"	*Paul Johnson*	SATB						
59	184	U	*Once in royal David's city*	5'30"	*Gauntlett/Mann/Wells*	SATB	S	2222	2231	Tp+3	Strings	NJBC
61	187	U	*On the First day (The Twelve Days of Christmas)*	3'40"	*Ian Humphris*	SSAATTBB	SB					NJBC
40	108	U	*Our Lady and Child (Lady, I sing to thee)*	1'40"	*Philip Moore*	SSATB						
18	43	U	*Our Lady's Lullaby (Dormi Jesu) (i)*	0'45"	*Philip Riley*	SSAA						
19	44	U	*Our Lady's Lullaby (Dormi Jesu) (ii)*	1'30"	*Richard R. Bennett*	SSAA						

No.	Cat.		Title	Dur.	Composer	Voicing	Solo					
62	195	U	*Past three o'clock* (London Waits) (i)	2'00"	*Charles Wood*	SATB						NJBC
63	196	U	*Past three o'clock* (London Waits) (ii)	3'00"	*William Llewellyn*	SSAATTBB	Br	2222	2231	Tp+2	Strings	NJBC
85	260	U	*Puer Nobis* (Unto us is born a Son)	2'00"	*William Llewellyn*	SATB						NJBC
64	200	U	*Rejoice and be merry* (A Gallery Carol)	1'30"	*Robin Wells*	SATB		2222	2231	Tp+2	Strings	NJBC
65	204		*Rejoice lordings*	0'50"	*Arthur Oldham*	SATB						
45	120	U	*Rocking Carol* (Mary's Child, so new and fair)	1'35"	*William Llewellyn*	SAATTBB						NJBC
54	160	U	*Sans Day Carol* (Now the holly bears a berry)	1'50"	*Ian Humphris*	SAATTBB						
44a	118	U	*Sant Josep i la Mare* (Mary, Mother of God's dear child)	1'30"	*Père Jorda*	SATB						
44b	119	U	*Sant Josep i la Mare de Deu*	1'30"	*Père Jorda*	SATB						
66	209	U	*See him born* (Il est né, le divin enfant)	2'00"	*William Llewellyn*	SSAATTBB		1200			Strings	NJBC
67	212	U	*See, to us a child is born* (A Christmas Antiphon) (i)	1'30"	*John Wilson*	SATB						
68	213		*See, to us a child is born* (A Christmas Antiphon) (ii)	1'30"	*John Wilson/W. Ll.*	SATB						
69	216	U	*Silent night* (Stille Nacht)	2'40"	*Ian Humphris*	SAATTBB						
70	218	U	*Sing lullaby!* (The Infant King)	1'45"	*William Llewellyn*	SATB						
50	140	U	*Sir Christemas* (Nowell, Nowell, Who is there?)	1'05"	*Robin Wells*	SATBB						
24	60	U	*Slumber Song of the Madonna* (Hushaby low)	2'00"	*Ronald Finch*	SAATTBB						
69	216	U	*Stille Nacht* (Silent night)	2'40"	*Ian Humphris*	SAATTBB						
4	6	U	*Susanni* (A little child there is yborn)	1'45"	*Ronald Corp*	SATB	S					
71	220	U	*Sweet was the song the Virgin sang* (Lute-book Lullaby)	2'15"	*Jeremy Thurlow*	SSAATTBB						
72	223	U	*The angel Gabriel* (Gabriel's message)	2'15"	*William Llewellyn*	SSAATTBB		1200			Strings	
73	226	U	*The Christ-child lay* (Carol of the Christ-child)	1'30"	*Philip Riley*	SATB						
74	228	U	*The first Nowell*	4'30"	*William Llewellyn*	SATB		2222	2231	Tp+2	Strings	NJBC
53	156		*The Golden Carol* (Now is Christemas ycome)	1'10"	*Paul Bendit*	SSAATTBB						
76	234		*The holly and the ivy*	2'45"	*William Llewellyn*	SSAATTBB	ST	2222	2231	Tp+2	Strings	NJBC
70	218	U	*The Infant King* (Sing lullaby!)	1'45"	*William Llewellyn*	SATB						
5	9	U	*The little road to Bethlehem* (As I walked down the road)	3'00"	*Michael Head*	SSAATTBB						
77	236	U	*The oak stands fast* (The Trees of the Field)	1'20"	*David Stone*	SATB						

NO.	PAGE	U	TITLE AND FIRST LINE (both are shown)	TIME	COMPOSER OR ARRANGER	VOICES Minimum Choir	Solo	Wind	Brass	Perc.	Strings	JUNIOR BOOK (NJBC)
11	23		The Oxen (Christmas Eve)	2'30"	Benjamin Britten	SA						
78	238	U	There is no rose of such virtue	2'00"	John Joubert	SATB						
79	240	U	The Shepherds' Farewell (Thou must leave)	3'30"	Hector Berlioz	SATB		0220			Strings	
28a	72	U	The Song of the Birds (In this most joyful night)	3'00"	Enrique Ribo	SATB						
77	236	U	The Trees of the Field (The oak stands fast)	1'20"	David Stone	SATB						
61	187	U	The Twelve Days of Christmas (On the First day)	3'40"	Ian Humphris	SSAATTBB	SB					NJBC
87	266	U	The Yorkshire Wassail (Wassail! We've been awhile)	3'00"	Ian Humphris	SSAATTBB	S/A					
79	240	U	Thou must leave (The Shepherds' Farewell)	3'30"	Hector Berlioz	SATB		0220			Strings	
80	244	U	Torches! (i)	1'40"	John Joubert	S or SA		2222	4231	Tp+1	Strings	NJBC
81	247	U	Torches! (ii)	1'40"	John Joubert	SATB		2222	4231	Tp+1	Strings	NJBC
26	66	U	Troc-a-tron (I'm a-ridin' to Bethlehem)	0'50"	Petr Eben	SATB						
82	250	U	'Twas in the moon of wintertime (Huron Carol)	1'50"	William Llewellyn	SSAATTBB						
84	256	U	Tyrle, tyrlow	1'45"	Healey Willan	SSAA						
85	260		Unto us is born a Son (Puer Nobis)	2'00"	William Llewellyn	SATB		2222	2231	Tp+2	Strings	NJBC
86	264	U	Villagers all, this frosty tide (Joy shall be yours)	1'30"	H. Fraser-Simson	SATB						
87	266	U	Wassail! We've been awhile (The Yorkshire Wassail)	3'00"	Ian Humphris	SSAATTBB	S/A					
83	253	U	What shall we give? (El Noi de la Mare)	1'50"	Enrique Ribo	SSAATTBB	S					
89	272	U	Whence is that goodly fragrance flowing? (i)	2'15"	William Llewellyn	TTBBB	T					
90	274	U	Whence is that goodly fragrance flowing? (ii)	2'15"	Robin Wells	SSATTBB						
88	270	U	Worship the Christ-child (Canon for three choirs)	1'30"	W. A. Mozart/W. Ll.	[SATB]×3						